Writer's Plight

Jake Thornton Ezell

Aperture Press

Copyright © 2016 by Jake Thornton Ezell.

All rights reserved. Published by Aperture Press. Name and associated logos are trademarks and/or registered trademarks of Aperture Press, LLC.

No part of this publication may be reproduced, stored in a retrieval system, or transmitted in any form or by any means, electronic, mechanical, photocopying, recording, or otherwise, without written permission of the publisher. For information, write to Aperture Press LLC, P.O. Box 6485, Reading, PA 19610 or visit www.AperturePress.net.

ISBN: 978-0-9973020-2-8

First Edition, 2016

Book designed by Sharon Wells Wagner.
Cover photo by Florian Klauer.
Author photo by Stephen Wagner.

*To the victims of Pompeii.
May you lay undisturbed.*

Contents

Author's Note	7
New Pen Zen	9
Drafter's Burden	11
Shakes While Reading	13
Committing Crimes	15
Tangible Remedy	17
Thirst	19
Inspiration	21
Plight of the Phyla Annelida	23
Significant Crustaceans	25
Swimming Away	27
A Prelude	29
Three-Fingered OJ	31
The Noise	33
To Have and Have Not a Poem	35
The Freudian Slip	37
The Rent is Due	39
Another Day in Paradise	41
Luxurious Materialism	43
I Am Your Classic 90s Bathroom	45
About the Author	47

Author's Note

This book is a look into my journey as a writer in a world overwhelmed by sound bites, click-bait, and bloggers fighting to remain at the top of relevance.

This book is about the writing process and personal growth I've experienced jotting down notes, feelings, and observations as I've tried to separate myself from the gyre of the world around me.

It's often an endeavor to create, express, and share when many are just trying to get by until the next paycheck, mile, or lover. It is a struggle. It is a journey. It is a process.

When I dug up and pieced together this short collection of poetry from 2009–2015 the theme of writing was apparent and the mood was strife.

This is *Writer's Plight.*

My writing goes AWOL, gets entombed and enshrined. Then it's time to start all over again.

New Pen Zen

On the ground
This new pen
Testing... Testing...
Thank Krishna,
it's blue.

Self-sufficiency is burdensome when
procrastination is seeded within
my own apprehensions.

Drafter's Burden

The rough draft of my
grocery list
sounds like: 30 minutes
of prep,
at least 5 minutes of
consideration,
2 minutes of inaction,
7 rational,
and a lifetime of regret
before considering it.
It's all just too far out there
to write down.

I caught a glimpse of myself in
the mirror when my mother brought out
the family photo album.

Shakes While Reading

You can see the arthritis in
his hands holding a
crumpled pack of
papers.

His fingers look sideways,
opposite of my own,
that are straight and
narrow,

Just like his were once,
when he was my age.

I'm conflicted between sharing and being my own backseat driver.

Committing Crimes

Leaving behind a chapbook makes
me feel scandalous,
Like I am committing the
worst crime
I'll ever be convicted
of.

Cigarettes are the channel
to put me down and tax twice.

Tangible Remedy

I pay more for the simple
convenience of
instant satisfaction for
things that
never last long.

When I run out of what I covet I devise,
before the calling comes.

Thirst

Sleep incompetence
has prompt
another Native cigarette

Which leaves
the eagerness
of answering the summons
of a soused individual's
last call.

I ate a cucumber.

I've never tried so hard to write
until I found myself, clueless.

Inspiration

Sitting in the Garden Chic
trying to identify 80,000
dollars
worth of plants
I realize, I
don't know shit
about plants.

I'll do anything to live one more slimy, meaningless moment.

Plight of the Phyla Annelida

An inclement day
on the saturated porch.
Indecent exposure of
the worms
gasping
for air.

(Originally published in
Canto Magazine, April 2014)

They gambled life away fishing in the wrong watering hole. Hook, line, and sinker.

Significant Crustaceans

Love
is like fishing for oysters:
The pearl
is inside—
maybe.

When I come across a fork
in the road, I take it.

Swimming Away

There's this thrill in life
that Fish requires.
There's this cupboard that is empty
in Fish's kitchen that desires
to be filled; Fish stuffs it full
of Fish's favorite eats—
canned corn, rice, books, humus,
chili, and beats.
Who knows what other things, but
it's always empty fore there
isn't enough time
left; Fish has been trying to bare
the waters rushing by
but prefers to flop on land best.

Competition became trivial when I witnessed beauty in cancer.

A Prelude

The players kick a stump
into the fire

Combusting amber and flame
into the heavenly bodies.

Look at her through its heat,
staring into the void
and all its emptiness.

Look at the conflagration flicker in her eyes
while the smoke from a
cancer-stick crawls out
her lips into the aether.

(Originally published in
Genesis Magazine, Fall 2012)

Yesterday pretended to be tomorrow today.

Three-Fingered OJ

Roll off the bed in taciturnity
to staggering toward the
kitchen fridge.

Repeat yourself.

Open the fridge and fix an
orange juice with a three-fingers,
and improvise so we may

start this dream all over again.

Knowingly or not, I've experienced many a fart in the wind from a Singapore butterfly.

The Noise

I am sound—
sturdy, strong, a tree in
the middle of a field.

I am secure, reliable, and
in good condition—beyond
mint—with callous scarrings.

I am sound—
the sensation and vibration through
the air and water, elastic,

a mechanical transmission, a
vocal utterance traveling 1,087 feet
per second at sea level.

I can hear the noise, the noise, noise,
Noise.

Even Hemingway in a dress couldn't
describe the resentment I've had.

To Have and Have Not a Poem

I would like to
put out a
collection of poetry—
a chapbook—
titled, "Cuckold: For My
Own Sake and
Every Other Man Involved."

Reminding myself my lover is not any more:
These are all good things.

The Freudian Slip

I made The Freudian Slip after headlines
motivated people not
to work and
coffee perked a second pot
already, then
her bowl of cereal was finished
and mine remained.

I made The Freudian Slip when screaming,
"You bitch, you
ruined my life,"
while her cereal soaked up
my milk.
I meant to say, "Could you pass
me the honey, babe."

(Originally published in
Canto Magazine, March 2013)

My life is a consistent open-mic governed
by some other master of ceremonies.

And The Rent is Due

The ends are tough, just like their
beginnings, but it's fear
of them coming and not the
dread of their arrival that
gets my blood churning during
the Gregorian calendar.

"Nothing is certain but death and taxes."
–Benjamin Franklin

"And spouses."
–Jake Thornton Ezell

Another Day in Paradise

☐ Electronic return originators...
Taxpayer's name: Jake Thornton Ezell
Spouse's name: _____
(Jointly filed return ONLY)
Purpose:
- For TE+Cos-66 must be completed...
General Instructions:
-Taxpayers must complete Part B before the...
DO NOT MAIL FORM TE+COS-66 TO THE TAX DEPARTMENT!

I lived on a houseboat for a time, both on land and off. Good enough.

Luxurious Materialism

Charmin filters
Gasoline-powered contact lenses
Take-out air conditioning
Hot water dryers
Colgate cable
Blu-ray movie tickets
Dishwasher sunglasses
Cell phone lighters
Automatic car wash doctors
A Urinal

When I must, I wonder how it became
plastic when I was bathed in cast-iron.

I Am Your Classic 90s Bathroom

"I am the grime that seeps from the
Septic tanks of suburban families
Signaling cashed checks
For a 2012 remodeling store…"

I am lying in a display tub, angry at
The year 2012.

"I can enjoy the nuance of 1999
Better… a people like me don't
Know why we cannot connect to
21st century nuances…"

I am standing in a display shower, angry at
The year 2013.

About the Author

Jake Thornton Ezell is from Mont Clare, Pennsylvania. The author of several works of poetry and nonfiction, his poems have been published in *Genesis* literary magazine, *Dead Flowers: A Poetry Rag*, *Field Notes: Interpretations of Nature,* and *Canto Magazine*. After graduation from college in the Midwest, Jake found himself back in Pennsylvania trying to figure out how to make a living with a degree in journalism.

CPSIA information can be obtained at www.ICGtesting.com
Printed in the USA
BVOW08s2210171016

465291BV00001B/33/P